MW00936327

THE POCKET GUIDE

to

SURVIVING LONELINESS

60 easy steps to follow

when you feel like

a complete weirdo

and a total failure

ELENA JDANOVA

ISBN: 1985650215
ISBN-13: 978-1985650213

DEDICATION

To my daughter, who courageously keeps finding her own steps on her own way.

To my friends, who help me find steps that are *mine*, and sometimes join me on my way.

CONTENTS

INTRODUCTION

This is a silly book. I had fun creating it, and I hope that you will have fun reading it. If on top of the fun you find some useful steps to practice, I will be beside myself with joy, because it is my intention to lift you out of the darkness, and into the light of a happier existence.

Most of the steps are obvious. I did not invent any wheels. But how often we overlook the obvious, as our emotional state slides downward! I hope that this book can be a reminder to take a positive action then.

You can use this guide in numerous ways.

- Read the steps one by one, or open a random page and contemplate the step that happens to be on that page

- Use the blank spaces and pages for your own notes. Scribble all you want--there is plenty of space provided for you

- Cut out your favorite page and stick it on your bathroom mirror, or carry it in your wallet, as a reminder

- Use a page to make an appropriate card for a friend you care about

- Be creative with the Guide--play as a child, grow into an adult you want to be

Reading it repeatedly including the notes you have added will be like hugging yourself. And believe me, you deserve big fat hug

Step 1

Congratulate yourself!

You have **already** accomplished Step 1. You picked up this *Guide* and, obviously, you are reading it. Now you can congratulate yourself for taking action! You don't know where the journey leads, but even one step is an exercise, and better than doing *nothing*.

Step 2

Remember that you deserve better,

and it's ***your responsibility*** to bring yourself to a better place. Even when drowning in darkness, try to pull yourself up like Baron Munchausen did, when he pulled himself out of a swamp by his own hair. (See step 50 for reference.)

Step 3

Make it your practice to always seek to improve your state.

Many individual **steps** become a journey that leads you **to a better place**.

Eventually.

Step 4

Start making some notes on the blank pages of this *Guide*.

Whatever comes to mind on the topic of loneliness is appropriate to record. **It's your book,** so it should **include your thoughts about your feelings and experiences**.

Start here:

Step 5

Don't assume everyone else is happy.

When you see everyone around **but yourself** as being happy-go-lucky, remember that either you **caught them at a good moment**, or they are **REALLY good at hiding their true feelings**. Like yourself, they are probably *scared to death* that somebody will notice their weirdness and inadequacy, and are trying to create a *smoke screen of being normal*.

Step 6

Breathe.

Not breathing will *not* make you appear less weird nor altogether *invisible*.

Plus, you might die from the lack of oxygen and then your friends or family will have to deal with the disposal of your dead body. *Not fair to them.*

You want to be fair; **being fair makes being visible more comfortable.**

Step 7

Consider your context.

Remember that you live in a **First World country**, and your feelings of loneliness and weirdness are mostly a **LUXURY**.

Those who live in the third world countries have to deal with much greater problems. *No bombs are falling on you.*

Step 8

Find your feet.

It will ensure you that **your head is not the only body part you have**.

And finding your feet will make it easier for you to take the next step.

Step 9

Go outside to get some sun and fresh air.

Boost your vitamin D level, clear the lungs and the head, and get a good-looking glow.

All of the above will **make you feel better**.

Step 10

Walk barefoot.

It will reinforce the connection to your **environment**, and give you more of a **sense of belonging**.

Your notes here (maybe about the best thing that
happened to you when you were in nature):

Step 11

Learn to **think intentionally**.

Lots of people have *habitual thoughts running freely* in their minds, triggering habitual emotional states they might not want.

Learn to recognize thoughts that are **not serving you** in any good way, and learn to **STOP** them. Replace them with positive thoughts.

- Recognize the looping thought that is pulling you down
- Stop that thought.
- Find a beneficial thought instead
- Replace the negative thought with the positive one

You can master the thought movement in your mind the way you've mastered the movements of your arms or legs.

Your notes here (maybe about what new thoughts will make **you** feel better):

Step 12

Normalize your abnormality.

You do not have nor do you experience anything that other people have never had or experienced. You are the product of your family and society, and all the ingredients you are made of came from somewhere. The reality you are experiencing is a **shared reality**, not unique to you only.

Your notes here (maybe about ways you consider yourself *weird* and who else you can think of who is also *weird* that way):

Step 13

When you feel like *a failure*, think of things you **don't want** to succeed at.

For example: you probably do not want to succeed at becoming the President of the United States and have to keep a straight face in front of Congress and the press every day while weird and bizarre things are happening all around the country... and maybe even in your head.

What else do you **NOT** want to be?

Step 14

Compare your failures and successes to **your own** failures and successes.

It's a *bad habit*, passed around too often, to compare your own failures to other people's successes. This is a sure way to destroy whatever little self-esteem you have left.

Instead, track your own highs and lows, your forward and backward movements. Success is anything that brought you satisfaction and improved the quality of your life.

Create your own scale and pace of progress, specific to your own abilities, sensitivities, needs, strengths and weaknesses. Was today better for you than yesterday or not?

Your notes here (maybe about the most recent success you have had; cooking a yummy dinner for a friend does count):

Step 15

Count your friends.

If you are able to count to **one**, know that you are lucky. Some people do not have even that.

Pick up the phone, call your friend, and ask them how they are doing. Invite them to go out for a beverage or a movie.

Step 16

Start taking responsibility for your life.

When you were a child, you did not have much control over how your parents should have been, where you lived, or what school you went to. Growing up means **recognizing more choices** around you and learning to **choose better**.

Growing up means taking care of your own self. After all, who else do you expect to do it?

Your notes here (maybe about what you are still waiting for someone else to provide for you):

Step 17

Learn to **recognize the feeling of hunger** and feed yourself as soon as you become aware of it.

Keep **good** snacks around. Cook **real** food.

The satisfaction of having something yummy in your tummy will push away the feeling of being miserable.

Step 18

Eat better food.

Junk food does not fill up "the hole," but only **creates more hunger** for more junk food.

Nourish yourself.

Step 19

Take a pill.

Aspirin is for a headache. Po Chai is for indigestion or a hangover. If you do not know what Po Chai is, research it on the Internet.

Even if you are a health nut, or do-it-all-yourself, or stick-it-out kind of person, take this option seriously. **If you can ease some of your misery, why not do it?**

Step 20

Stop taking pills.

That is, if you take too many too often.

Drop the crutches, **exercise walking on your own two legs**, so to speak.

But be practical and do it the right way. Consult your physician, as they often say.

Your notes here (maybe about how your current state of health might be affecting your state of mind):

Step 21

Get some sleep.

Tomorrow will be another day.

Step 22

Masturbate.

A little pleasure goes a long way.

Step 23

Wash the dirty dishes.

They attract flies, mold and microbes. Even though on a bad day *they seem like company*, their excessive presence weakens your immune system, which makes you *fail* more often, which kills your self-esteem. And then the foul smell makes the foul mood much fouler.

Step 24

Do the laundry.

Wearing **fresh** smelling clothes will **boost** your self-esteem and make it easier for another human being to approach you.

Step 25

Take the garbage **out.**

Cleanliness is next to godliness.

Your notes here (maybe start a 'to do" list):

Step 26

Get rid of what you don't need.

Go through your closets and pull out clothes that you have not been wearing for the last year or more. Then put back the special occasion clothes–like for a funeral, a wedding or a job interview (believe me, there will come a day when you'll be grateful you've kept those clothes).

Take the rest of the pile to a clothing donation drop box (if you are lucky to live in a progressive place like California), to a resale store, or just put it out on the curb with a big "*FREE*" sign.

Recycling (any kind of recycling or donating) **makes you a part of** the longer environmental chain of conservation and broadens your world. In other words, recycling makes you a part of **something bigger than the little every day you** that you are sometimes so tired of.

Step 27

Clean your house.

Clean the floors and the furniture surfaces. Clean the kitchen—the counters, the fridge, the stove top. Put things in order. Make the space nice.

It's a Zen thing: **making your home ready to receive a visit from God**. From all imaginary friends you can have, God is the best one. He can be whatever you want him to be, and can be more than that. He can be a She, too. Or an "it" simply called Spirit.

Making your home nice invites God's good side, or "**good energy**." Believe me, you do want God, imaginable or real, **to be your friend**.

Step 28

Buy fresh flowers for your home.

Put up lovely **"impressions"** that are meaningful and beautiful to you. Try art pieces, rock crystals or maybe ornate pillows.

Impressions are food for your eyes and heart. Make it be *good* visual food. Be intentional in decorating your home.

Your notes here (maybe about what changes can make your home a more uplifting environment for you):

Step 29

Get a **cat**.

Cats are excellent companions, and **great teachers of contentment** because most cats are perfectly content simply *being*.

If you happen to have the misfortune of living with a neurotic cat that is asking for your attention all the time, or yells and scratches furniture to protest your absence, take a step in the opposite direction. Give that cat away. The quality of your alone time will increase tremendously then because you will not be spending so much energy on someone else's unreasonable neediness.

Let it go. It's that simple.

Step 30

Share a ride instead of driving your own car everywhere.

There are sites all over the Internet which make ride-sharing safe. Lots of people are looking for company or to share the cost of the drive. The environment and everything living in it **will improve** from having less pollution. That's **empowerment**.

Step 31

Stop and give someone a ride.

Hitchhikers might look weird so use your **good judgement** about which person you would be scared to open the door of your car for and which one is **harmless**.

Once I gave ride to a whole family: a woman in her 40s, her boyfriend, her 16 year old son, and their dog. They were fun and good people, and told interesting stories about their ten plus years on the road.

Your notes here (maybe about how you feel about talking to strangers):

Step 32

Sing!

Join a choir. Singing together is a **miraculous opportunity** to disappear yourself while joining your voice with other voices in harmony.

If you are not a singer for an audience, be a singer for yourself—in the shower, at the woods, on an empty hilltop.

Amazingly satisfying! This activity is useful for promoting pain relief physically, emotionally, and spiritually.

Your notes here about kinds of music or songs that uplift you:

Step 33

Take a class.

Take a class about cooking, or yoga, or motorcycle repair, or **anything!** You might not have to own your own motorcycle to go to that class, but think of all the **cool people** you might meet, bonding with them over various motorcycle parts. And having a class scheduled on your calendar **will make you get out of the house and be with other people on a regular basis.**

Step 34

Take a class where you'd have to partner up with someone.

Like a ballroom dancing class. Now that's **advanced!** You'll have to deal not only with integrating the new material the class teaches, but with your partner's ability (or dis-ability) to integrate that same material.

The good part is that, if all goes well, it might be **easier to take that new partner out** to lunch or dinner, and then who knows what happens, if you are catching my drift... And in a worst case partner scenario, you can ditch them at the end of the class, or even summon the courage to ask for a different partner.

Step 35

Take a class or a workshop on **communication**, on **relationships**, or on **dealing with feelings**.

Maybe you'll be lucky to find a good class on *loneliness*. You'll find other lonely people there and you'll see clearly that you are not alone in experiencing this feeling. You'll practice the togetherness of lonely people, which is awesome, and **happens naturally in life anyhow**.

If you won't be able to find a class on loneliness, **you can start your own personal class just for you, and *invent anti-loneliness exercises to perform every day!***

Your notes here (maybe about class subjects that interest you):

Step 36

Invent your own "steps" that help you feel better.

Use the blank pages of this book to write them down. Post the list on your Facebook page or in some other **social media** you like. Post it somewhere others will find it, like **The Guide page on Facebook.**

Let's make this book a community project!

Your notes here (maybe about steps that make you feel better):

Step 37

Go to church.

Follow this step with caution and make your own judgement, based on your observation and experience. If you are tired of looking for God alone and want company, Church is an option.

Discern between wanting the company of other God-seekers and the company of God.

In my experience God shows Him/Her/Itself when one is **seeking intensely**, alone or not alone.

Step 38

Practice *intentional alone-ness*.

Find ways to *savor* alone time with a movie, a book, balancing your check-book or journaling.

High quality leisure or purposeful alone time is *priceless* and *good for you*!

Step 39

Write a book (Like this one right here).

It's a **step up** from talking with an imaginary friend. It takes your mind off your loneliness, and at the end of the process there is a human being (like yourself) reading your written words. Even if you'll have only one reader, it's worth it. But then, if there will be one, **there will be more**.

Write some possible topics you would like to write about here:

Step 40

Invent or make something--gadgets, devices, machines, etc.

Perhaps your creativity is blocked by low self-esteem. **Unblock your creativity.** Give yourself permission to create things (or paintings, or songs) even if only a few people are likely to understand or appreciate them.

Your creations might be outside-of-the-box or not utilized right away, but eventually a great way to **share them with someone who needs them** might present itself. As your creativity evolves and finds ways to be expressed, it will help you **create a new, *better* identity**, and will continue to serve you in the future.

Step 41

Go to a crowded place like a park or a busy commercial street.

Find a bench to sit on, be invisible in plain sight, and watch people. Observe all different ways they move, talk, laugh, drink coffee; their facial expressions, clothes...

Soak in lots of human presence.

Step 42

Talk to a therapist.

Many therapists are wounded healers who know trauma and its effects on the human psyche from personal experience. And they do have **training** to help you **become a more balanced, happier, and more fufilled person.** You might have to go through a few therapists to find the right one for you, the one you can trust and form a healing relationship with, but it's worth the effort.

Be careful not to expect them to be your parent or lover. A therapist might counsel you about your relationship needs, but that's where their role ends.

Step 43

Consider a house share.

Living with other human beings who are not blood relatives gives you more freedom to **socialize with them on your own terms**, as in only when you want to. Otherwise you can just go to your room and close the door behind you.

But choose your housemates wisely. Avoid people who would barge through your closed door any time of day or night, or who bring other people in who make loud noises that go right through your closed door.

Step 44

Feel your feelings.

Not just those you **want to feel**. Feel *all of them.* Sit with them, meditate with them. ***Own them.*** All your feelings are part of your human experience. You can find the way to make them your friends, your guides, and your teachers.

List some of your feelings here:

Step 45

Deepen your conversations.

You might **discover a more real person** behind the happy-go-lucky facade, someone with their own loneliness, weirdness and insecurity. Believe it or not, *you are not the lone holder of those qualities in this world.*

Step 46

Listen.

Not just to your own thoughts, but **to what others have to say**. Listen *deeper,* beyond the superficiality of casual words exchanged.

Listening will take your mind off your own misery and will help you focus beyond yourself.

Step 47

Talk to your neighbor.

You will not necessarily find a friend there, but **a possibility to ease a small crisis** like, for example, discovering that you are out of salt in the middle of your chili cooking and are unable to go to the grocery store right at that moment.

You'll gain at least two easy casual human connections out of that situation if you first borrow something and then return it to that neighbor. *Easy!* And more and more easy each time.

Step 48

Share.

Bring an extra snack and share it with a co-worker. Cook extra food and invite your neighbor to share the meal. Or give it away to a homeless person.

Be creative about what you can share, and write down some ideas here:

Step 49

Grow your own food.

A couple of tomatoes, a lettuce or a kale plant will make you a part of the vast gardening community. You can find other people who are eager to visit each other's gardens for learning and inspiration, or are eager to meet for a seeds or seedlings exchange. And sometimes you'll get an extra chance to visit that neighbor of yours again to give away your extra zucchinis or cucumbers.

Even if you are a lone gardener in the middle of a community which gets all their food from a grocery store, **growing your own food will increase your sense of belonging to your environment and reduce the sense of loneliness and weirdness**.

Trust me; it works that way.

Step 50

Find a good book to read.

Like *The Surprising Adventures of Baron Munchausen* by Rudolf Erich Raspe. **Better to lose yourself in a fun story than stay trapped in a funky state.** There are lots of suggested reading lists out there at the library or online. Find one.

Your notes here about your favorite titles or genres:

Step 51

Give hugs.

It might feel totally uncomfortable at first. Why hug those weird people? Don't think about them. **You are going to do it for you.**

Here is a break-down of the process: ask for permission to hug, receive the permission. *Hug.* Close your eyes, tune them out, and tune into your own heart. Think something appropriate, like, **"It's okay, everything is okay."** Take a breath. Disengage from the embrace. Put your hand on your chest and say "Thank you."

Make it a practice. One random hug is not going to change anything, but the practice will.

Step 52

Breed dogs and sell puppies.

Puppies are a **happy presence**, and meeting people over a puppy sale is a happy event. Puppies, and dogs in general, though, require space and care. They will chew your shoes, computer cables and rugs. You can breed hamsters instead. Or propagate orchids. Or get a job at a pet store or a petting zoo. **Even better, volunteer at an animal shelter.** Same idea.

You will find **plenty of easy and positive opportunities for socialization** when you spend time with living beings other than humans.

Your notes here:

Step 53

Start looking for a better job.

Better job conditions or better pay will boost your confidence, reduce your anxiety and will make you feel more adequate.

Step 54

Become an expert in something.

People will come to you for your expertise and you can be weird all you want. Actually, people will **feel less inferior** with a weirdo expert. They will feel more relaxed and more forgiving around you if you are a *weird* expert (versus a "*superior*" person).

Step 55

Get a job in the service industry.

Become a bartender, an auto glass installer, or a receptionist. Again, **people will come to you all the time**, and at the end of the day your alone time will not be loneliness, but a *blessing*.

Step 56

Get a serious in-depth book on the psychology of loneliness.

Educate yourself because **education is power**.

Step 57

Study **your own psychology** and belief systems.

Become an expert in **knowing yourself** and a master of practices that will allow you to become a more balanced, fulfilled, and happier person.

Save the world by saving yourself!

Step 58

Understand yourself better.

Remember that a lot of disconnection, resulting in feelings of loneliness, is *your own doing*. Somehow, deep in your psyche, you decided that *company is not for you*, and you *positioned yourself separately*.

Own your choice.

Learn to *choose* to join in… or to stay apart from others… *intentionally*.

Step 59

Expect periodic set-backs.

Remember that no matter how much you **work on yourself**, trying to change your behavioral patterns, or your relationships with your feelings and with the people around you, **there will be time and time again when the old feelings of loneliness and inadequacy will return**.

It may be even *harder* to experience these feelings because of all the work you put into improving yourself. You may judge yourself hard, feeling that all your efforts are failing. That kind of judgement is not helpful.

Pause, breathe, and wait for the moment (hour, day, or week) to pass. ***It will pass, and your state will get better.***

Step 60

Pay attention to the moments **when you do feel good**.

Normalize these moments, attach your identity to the good feelings, stretch them, **do everything you can** to make it a *new base* of normality for yourself.

Your notes here (maybe about what you plan to do next):

ABOUT THE AUTHOR

Elena Jdanova is a Russian-born writer living in California. Her journey of self-exploration has been life-long over six decades and included crossing many boundaries of different countries, cultures and relationships. She has grown to understand that aloneness is not just loneliness, but is another side of togetherness.

Elena's other stories are fables about the magical character Hank, all collected in the latest edition of "Tales of Hank." These tales for adults talk about love and unexpected twists of relationships, when people with different gifts meet each other.

Elena Jdanova